Super Fun

Road Trip Activities

for Kids

Super Fun Road Trip Activities for Kids is an original work, first published in 2022 by Fox Chapel Publishing Company, Inc. Reproduction of its contents is strictly prohibited without written permission from the rights holder.

ISBN 978-1-64124-240-0

To learn more about the other great books from Fox Chapel Publishing, or to find a retailer near you, call toll-free 800-457-9112 or visit us at *www.FoxChapelPublishing.com*.

We are always looking for talented authors. To submit an idea, please send a brief inquiry to acquisitions@foxchapelpublishing.com.

Fox Chapel Publishing makes every effort to use environmentally friendly paper for printing.

Printed in China
First printing

Super Fun Road Trip Activities for Kids

Vicki Whiting
Illustrated by
Jeff Schinkel

Happy Fox
BOOKS

"I haven't been everywhere, but it's on my list."

— SUSAN SONTAG

Super Fun Road Trip

Family Road Trip

The Wheeler family has piled into the car to go on an exciting road trip to Lake Puddleston. Along the way, they want to see the following sites and attractions:

- ☐ Cactus Pointe Park
- ☐ Giant Gumball Pyramid
- ☐ Tasty Soup Factory Tour

Find the route that uses the least amount of fuel, while still seeing those sites, by finding the lowest total along the roadway. Don't go back over any of the roads you've already traveled.

License Plate Literacy

Some cars have personalized license plates. Can you figure out what each one below means? Write your answers underneath each license plate. Then ask a family member to check your work.

SML 4 ME

S M _ _ L _
_ _ O _ _ M E

AWSM TCHR

_ _ _ _ _ _ _
_ _ _ _ _ _ _

UR GR8

_ _ _
_ _ _ _

LV 2 TRVL

_ _ _ _
_ _ _ _ _ _

GD 2B ME

_ _ _ _ _ _
_ _ _ _ _

FUN 2 LRN

_ _ _ _
_ _ _ _ _

DRM BIGR

_ _ _ _ _

HAP E KDZ

_ _ _ _ _
_ _ _ _

7

North American Road Trip

When people take long drives in North America, they need to make stops for rest and food. Over the years, businesses have come up with curious and odd attractions to get people to stop at their stores and restaurants. Unscramble the letters to find out in which American state or Canadian Province each is located.

The World's Largest Ball of Twine was started in 1953. It weighs more that 19,000 pounds and is over 1,500 miles long. You can see it in **SANAKS**

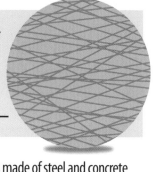

_ _ _ _ _ _

Nearly 10 metres tall, Mac the Moose is made of steel and concrete weighing 9,000 kg (nearly 19,842 pounds!) in the Canadian province of

SAKATCHENAWS

_ _ _ _ _ _ _ _ _ _ _ _

A 120-foot-tall baseball bat leans against the Louisville Slugger Museum in this state.

CUYEKTNK

_ _ _ _ _ _ _ _

Cadillac Ranch is a row of 10 cars stuck nose-first into the ground in the state of

STAXE

_ _ _ _ _

Color these cars.

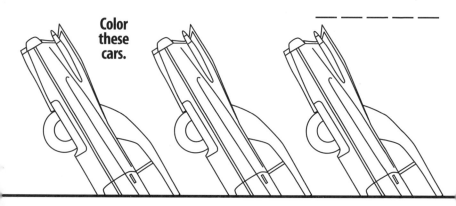

In the city of Scappoose, the 50-foot-tall Peace Candle of the World was created in 1971 by covering a farm silo with 45,000 lbs. of red candle wax. It has a neon flame today, but was originally lit with a giant 60-foot-long match! It is located in the state of

ROONEG

___ ___ ___ ___ ___ ___

In the 1930s, Douglas Herrick and his brothers, put deer antlers onto a jackrabbit carcass and called it a Jackalope. They sold it to a hotel in

MOWINGY

___ ___ ___ ___ ___ ___ ___

A 50-foot-high slingshot is carved from a dead poplar tree in this Canadian province.

UCQBEE

___ ___ ___ ___ ___ ___

Which kind of artist draws funny pictures of motor vehicles?

ANSWER: A car-toonist.

The World's Longest Maze

In this state, you can walk through a huge maze made up of over 14,000 colorful, tropical plants. Unscramble the letters along the correct path to discover the name of this state.

_____ __ _____ __ __ ___ _____

Minivan Matchup

Look closely! Find the two identical minivans.

Jumbo Word Search

Find the words by looking up, down, backwards, forwards, sideways, and diagonally.

```
E  E  S  U  O  I  R  U  C  D
N  P  T  R  A  D  D  S  L  T
I  O  O  R  E  E  O  I  D  H
W  L  P  D  V  H  C  E  O  G
T  A  S  R  D  E  T  T  I  I
A  K  A  A  N  A  E  A  D  E
L  C  T  S  C  L  N  R  F  W
L  A  E  O  I  T  I  S  I  V
P  J  L  S  R  E  L  T  N  A
```

JACKALOPE	ANTLERS	VISIT
LICENSE	WEIGHT	HOTEL
FATHERS	CARVED	STOPS
LOCATED	TWINE	TALL
CURIOUS	GIANT	ODD

Road Trip Journal

DATE:

PLACES WE WENT:

WHAT WE DID:

MY FAVORITE MEMORY OF THE DAY:

FUN AT THE FAIR

Long ago ...

Farm families came to sell their goods and proudly display their best produce, stitchery, canned goods, and animals.

Fairs were also a place to hear speakers and music and get up and dance. People took turns at the midway games to show off their strength.

Covered Wagons

Baking
Competitions

Today ...

Members of 4-H clubs show the animals they have raised and compete for recognition. Popular animal competitions include sheep, pigs, calves, and chickens, as well as llamas. People play modern midway games and line up to go on roller coasters, Ferris wheels, and other rides.

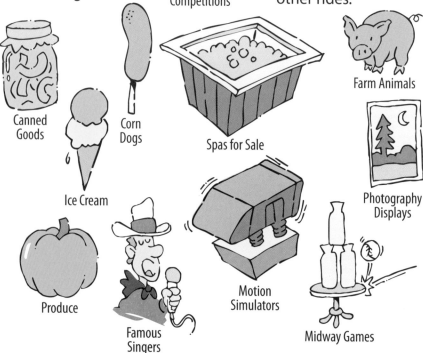

Canned
Goods

Corn
Dogs

Spas for Sale

Farm Animals

Ice Cream

Photography
Displays

Produce

Famous
Singers

Motion
Simulators

Midway Games

Now & Then

Pictured on page 14 are items found at fairs over the years. In the circle at the top, write the names of items that could only be found at fairs 100 years ago. In the circle on the bottom, list things you could only find at a fair today.

Where the two ovals overlap, write the names of items you could find at fairs today AND in the past. Can you think of things to add to each group?

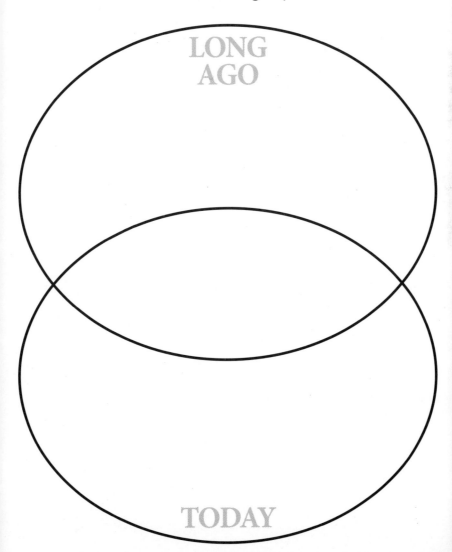

LONG AGO

TODAY

Katie and Nathan played the Balloon Pop game on the
fair's midway. Katie popped all the odd-numbered balloons.
Nathan popped all the even-numbered balloons.
Add up each. Who got the highest score?

Livestock Scramble

People bring their finest livestock to fairs. Unscramble the words below each person to find out which animal he or she brought to the fair.

GPI

OWC

TRIBAB

MALB

TEUKYR

ENKICCH

What did the farmer say to the cow who refused to go to sleep?

ANSWER: "Hey, it's pasture bedtime!"

Who won the Pie Baking Contest?

Here are the top three pies in the fair's Annual Pie Baking Contest. Use the judge's secret code to add up each pie's score. Write in 1st, 2nd, or 3rd place on each pie's ribbon. Color the 1st place ribbon blue.

◣ = 2   ➕ = 6
★ = 3   ◪ = 7
◿ = 4   ◣ = 8
⊢ = 5   ✖ = 9

Judge's Score Card

Color	➕
Aroma	✖
Texture	◪
Flavor	✖
TOTAL	

Judge's Score Card

Color	⊢
Aroma	◿
Texture	◣
Flavor	➕
TOTAL	

Judge's Score Card

Color	◪
Aroma	◣
Texture	➕
Flavor	✖
TOTAL	

Draw in the missing squares to finish the pattern on this quilt for the fair.

Jumbo Word Search

Find the words by looking up, down, backwards, forwards, sideways, and diagonally.

```
E X H I B I T S C E
S C E E D A R T C L
L L N E B Y A U F F
L O R A A R D A L E
A C E W D O I R I R
H K D A R R T D N R
T I O P S E I S E I
M T M Y A D O T A S
T S L A M I N A E S
```

FAIRS	MODERN	RIDES
TRADITION	MIDWAY	TRADE
PRODUCE	FERRIS	HALLS
ANIMALS	DANCE	TODAY
EXHIBITS	CLOCK	LINE

Road Trip Journal

DATE:

PLACES WE WENT:

WHAT WE DID:

MY FAVORITE MEMORY OF THE DAY:

Water Park Fun!

Water parks are great fun in the summertime. Thrilling, twisty water slides, relaxing lazy rivers, and spraying fountains that drench you in cool water make for the perfect place to spend a summer vacation day.

But you need to be careful so you don't get too much sun! Too much sun can cause a painful burn and even increase your chances of skin cancer.

How many sunglasses can you find on this page?

Protect Your Skin!

Replace the missing vowels to discover how to protect your skin from burning at a water park.

W_ _R
A
H_T

W_ _RA
SH_RT
OVER
Y_ _R
SW_M S_ _T

ST_Y
_N THE
SH_D_

SPF 50

USE
S_NSCR_ _N

Wild Water Slides

Can you figure out where each water slide begins and ends?
Write the correct letter at the end of each slide.

Amazing Water Parks

Do the math to discover amazing facts about these water parks!

The Wisconsin Dells boasts more than twenty indoor and outdoor water parks. They hold a combined total of _____ $8 + 2 + 6$ million gallons of water.

Noah's Ark, located in the Dells, is America's largest water park. It covers _____ $47 + 23$ acres with three miles of water slides.

A water slide at the Atlantis resort in the Bahamas features a _____ $29 + 31$ foot slide with a clear tube through a shark pool!

The world's largest indoor wave pool is in Edmonton, Canada. The tropical oasis there has an average temperature of _____ $9 + 22$ °C (88°F).

Deep River Waterpark in Indiana has its own ice-skating rink. You must be _____ $33 + 13$ inches tall to ride the Dragon Speed Rides.

Cedar Point Shores Waterpark in Sandusky, Ohio has a ride with a _____ $22 - 16$ story drop where riders free fall to the pool below.

How many pool noodles do you see?

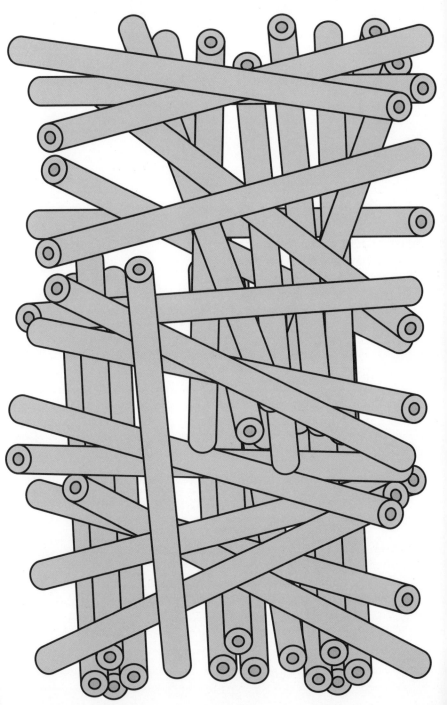

Make Your Own Water Park

If you can't make it to a water park, try making your own water playground in your back yard or at a local park. Here are some ideas!

Juggle or toss water balloons.

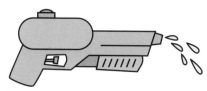

Create a squirt gun shower. Squirt water out of the gun and over your head and see if you can turn around two times before the water hits the ground.

Play a water balloon head catch game by taping a plastic mixing bowl to the top of a bike or batting helmet. One person throws the balloon and the other one tries to catch it in the bowl. Lots of splashes guaranteed!

Play baseball and/or basketball with water balloons instead of balls!

Always remember to collect broken water balloons at the end of your game and put them in the trash.

What's the most popular TV show in the ocean?

ANSWER: Whale of Fortune.

Water Workouts

Gather some friends and try playing some of these games.

They're good exercise and a great way to beat the heat!

Water Balloon Freeze Tag

The person who is IT must protect a bucket filled with water balloons. If other players get soaked by a water balloon, even if one drop hits them, they must remain frozen until another player is able to snatch a water balloon from the bucket and unfreeze them by soaking them with it!

Sponge Volley

String a rope between two trees. Hang a tarp so that players can't see the other side of the court. Have full water buckets and big sponges on each side. Toss soaked sponges over to the other side to see if you can hit the other players.

Jumbo Word Search

Find the words by looking up, down, backwards, forwards, sideways, and diagonally.

```
S  N  I  S  N  O  C  S  I  W
P  L  I  S  H  A  O  N  S  A
S  H  I  R  H  W  L  O  N  V
P  E  G  E  A  A  A  L  N  E
L  D  D  V  T  T  P  L  D  S
A  S  W  I  M  E  P  A  L  A
S  S  P  R  L  R  H  G  R  H
H  A  Q  U  A  S  I  N  G  K
C  L  A  G  O  O  N  F  U  N
```

WISCONSIN	RIVERS	PARK
GALLONS	LAGOON	SWIM
CAPITAL	WATER	WAVE
SLIDES	NOAHS	AQUA
SPLASH	SHADE	HAT

Road Trip Journal

DATE:

PLACES WE WENT:

WHAT WE DID:

MY FAVORITE MEMORY OF THE DAY:

A Walk in the Woods

A forest is filled with interesting things to see, hear, feel, and do. This road trip takes you on an adventure in the woods.

ANIMAL GROUPS

What do you call a group of these woodland animals? Circle every other letter under each animal to discover the answer!

PORCUPINES

RASPDRNI
RCZKTLME

A _ P _ _ _ _

SKUNKS

JAFSMUWR
PFYEUIVT

_ _ _ _ _ _

SQUIRRELS

DALSMCOU
YRKRTY

_ _ _ _ _ _

FOXES

TAPLQEN
AKSVH

_ _ _ _ _

ELK

CADGTA
HNBG

_ _ _ _ _

BATS

HATCPOGL
BOENRY

_ _ _ _ _

Woods Watcher

Look closely at this picture of the woods.
Can you find each of the following?

- ❏ mushroom
- ❏ bird nest
- ❏ animal track
- ❏ spider web
- ❏ bird feather

- ❏ two caterpillars
- ❏ moss
- ❏ five butterflies
- ❏ acorn
- ❏ six ladybugs

Camp Confusion

Find the two identical camp scenes.

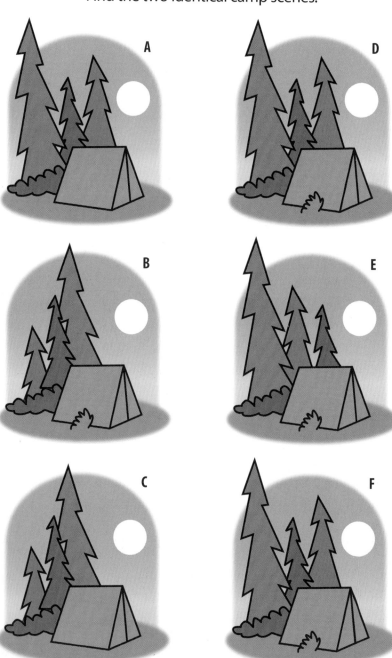

Put Out That Campfire!

There's nothing like a cozy campfire after a long day in the woods. But you have to make sure your campfire is all the way out before going to sleep. Get this bucket of water to the campfire to put it completely out!

START ▶

FINISH

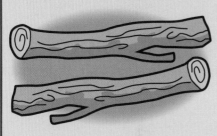

How do you start a campfire using just two pieces of wood?

ANSWER: Make sure one is a matchstick.

Who is walking in the woods?

Match each animal to its footprint.
Do the math to check your answers.

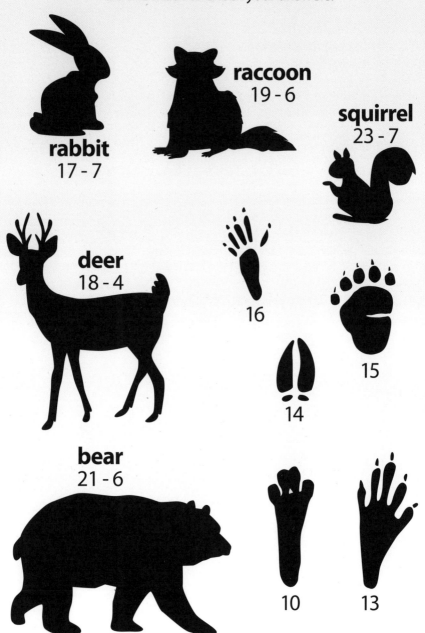

rabbit
17 - 7

raccoon
19 - 6

squirrel
23 - 7

deer
18 - 4

16

15

14

bear
21 - 6

10

13

General Sherman Tree is a Record Breaker!

The General Sherman Tree, located in Sequoia National Park, is not only the largest living tree, **it is the largest living thing,** by volume, on the planet. Use the code to find out more about it.

The tree is estimated to be

___ ___ ___ ___ years old.

It weighs ___ ___ ___ tons.

It's ___ ___ ___ feet (83m) tall.

The distance around the bottom of the tree is

___ ___ ___ feet (31m).

It has branches that are

almost ___ feet (2.1m) in diameter.

CODE

0 = ◒
1 = ◀
2 = ★
3 = ◐
4 = ▶
5 = ♥
6 = ◖
7 = ▲
8 = ◎
9 = ●

The **largest** tree in the world is the General Sherman. It is a **giant sequoia** and measures in volume 52,508 cubic feet. A cubic foot is a cube one foot wide by one foot tall by one foot deep.

1 foot
1 foot
1 foot

Jumbo Word Search

Find the words by looking up, down, backwards, forwards, sideways, and diagonally.

```
E E E R E D I P S X
N D R I B R E E D P
I E M U S H R O O M
P L E O T R E K O N
U A N R T N C U W N
C R E H T A E F E R
R R S N R A L V B O
O L T T I O W O D C
P O D L W P A N D A
```

ADVENTURE	TRACK	TREE
PORCUPINE	WOODS	BIRD
MUSHROOM	ACORN	NEST
FEATHER	WOLF	DEER
SPIDER	PINE	WEB

Road Trip Journal

DATE:

PLACES WE WENT:

WHAT WE DID:

MY FAVORITE MEMORY OF THE DAY:

A Day at the Zoo

How Hippos Keep Their Cool

To stay cool in the African heat, hippos spend most of their day in rivers and lakes. Their eyes, nose and ears are located on the top of their head, which means they can see and breathe while the rest of their body is underwater.

Danger!

Don't let their gentle appearance fool you. The hippopotamus is considered the world's deadliest large land mammal. These giants kill an estimated 500 people per year in Africa.

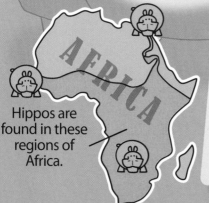

Hippos are found in these regions of Africa.

Hippos leave the water at night to look for food. They like to eat grass—lots of grass. They eat 80 lbs (35 kg) of vegetation each night.

Circle every other letter to discover what the name *hippopotamus* means.

W**R**J I A V L E Y R G H P O A R T S M E

R _ _ _ _   _ _ _ _ _

38

Monkey See, Monkey Do

Sometimes, monkeys like to imitate each other! Look at these monkeys to find the two that are exactly the same.

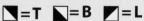

Tiny and Cute!

Chameleon Cutie

The world's smallest chameleon, the *Brookesia micra* **chameleon** lives on the island of Madagascar.

Adult males grow to only about a half-inch (16 millimeters) from nose to tail. This chameleon is so small that you might miss it if you don't look very closely. In fact, scientists did miss this tiny guy for a long time.

Circle every third number to discover the year the *Brookesia micra* chameleon was discovered.

7 1 (2) 4 9 0 3 7 1 5 1 2

2 __ __ __

Dwarf Three-Toed Jerboa

The **dwarf three-toed jerboa** is the world's smallest rodent. It weighs less than an ounce and is about 1.7 inches tall. Jerboas live in deserts and dry areas in North Africa and Asia, where they dig underground burrows.

Some people compare its little body to a:

☒ ★ ◨ ◨ ★ ◪ ◨ ◉ ◪ ◪

◉ = A   ☒ = C   ◪ = N   ◨ = T   ◩ = B   ◪ = L   ★ = O   ✓ = S

What are Pangolins?

Pangolins are found in Asia and Africa.

Reptile or Mammal?

Study this sketch of a pangolin carefully. Read the description of reptiles and mammals and decide if pangolins are mammals or reptiles. Then use the code to check your answer.

Reptiles

A reptile is a cold-blooded animal that breathes air and usually has skin covered with scales or bony plates. Snakes, lizards, turtles, and alligators are reptiles.

Mammals

A mammal is a warm-blooded animal with a backbone that feeds its young with milk produced by the mother and has skin usually more or less covered with hair. Dogs, mice, bears, whales, and human beings are mammals.

Pangolins are __ __ __ __ __ __ __ .

⊠ ◨ ⊠ ⊠ ◨ ◩ ⊠

◨=A ★=E ◪=I ⬠=P ⊠=S ⊡=C ◩=L ⊠=M ▯=R ⬒=T

Which giraffe is the tallest?

Convert the size of each giraffe into feet to find out!

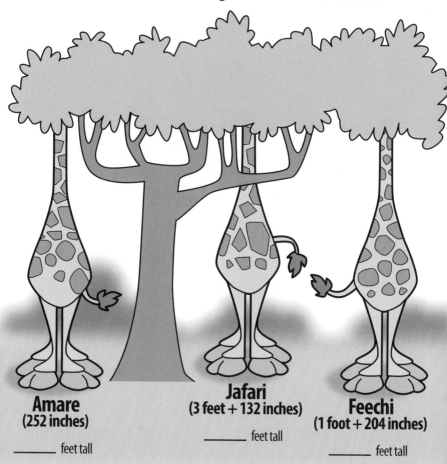

Amare
(252 inches)

_____ feet tall

Jafari
(3 feet + 132 inches)

_____ feet tall

Feechi
(1 foot + 204 inches)

_____ feet tall

Why is it so difficult to fool a snake?

ANSWER: You can't pull their leg.

Ask a Tasmanian Devil

Q: Why are you called devils?

A: That's a great question! Tasmanian devils aren't dangerous to people. We're actually shy animals.

The name "devil" may come from the sounds we make. We make eerie growls at night when looking for food. I guess it scares some folks. Sorry! We can't help it.

Q: What do Tasmanian devils eat?

A: We are **carnivores**. That means we eat _____. And we're also **scavengers**, which means we mostly eat dead or dying animals we _____.

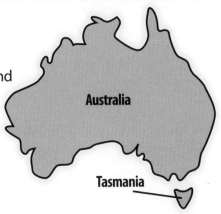

Zoom! Crunch! It's time for lunch!

_____ believe that Tasmanian devils were once good runners. But since the _____ of cars, we get plenty of food by eating the animals that get run over. So, we don't have to cover large _____ searching for food like we did back in the old days.

DISTANCES

SCIENTISTS

INVENTION

FIND   MEAT

Q: Where do Tasmanian devils live?

A: We live on an Australian island called Tasmania. At one time, we lived throughout mainland Australia.

About 400 years ago we disappeared from the Australian mainland.

Australia

Tasmania

Jumbo Word Search

Find the words by looking up, down, backwards, forwards, sideways, and diagonally.

```
N O I T C N I T X E
A N I M A L C O H M
N C C O N D O R O P
D L I W F I S N P I
E E W R R S K V E R
A D O T F E G G S E
I G R O Y A D O T N
S E L S I S O O Z S
K E D Y Y E L L O W
```

EXTINCTION   CONDOR   TODAY
DISEASE   ANIMAL   ZOOS
MONKEYS   YELLOW   EGGS
AFRICA   FROGS   WILD
EMPIRE   WORLD   EDGE

Road Trip Journal

DATE: _____

PLACES WE WENT: _____

_____

_____

_____

WHAT WE DID: _____

_____

_____

_____

_____

_____

_____

_____

_____

_____

_____

MY FAVORITE MEMORY OF THE DAY: _____

_____

_____

_____

_____

_____

_____

A Day at the Beach

It's a beautiful day at the seashore. Dive deep and take a close look at this school of fish. Only one of them is different from all the rest. Can you find it?

Bummer, dude!

Can you help this surfer find his way to the water without crushing the little kid's sand castles?

Surfboard Scramble

Can you find the two surfboards that match?

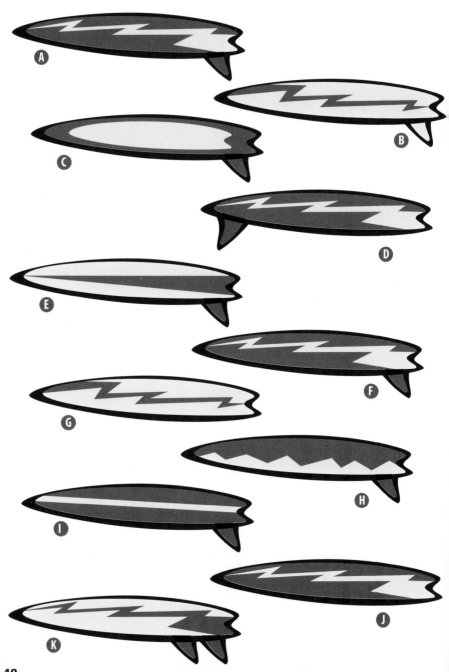

Super Sea-cret Message

Unscramble the mixed-up words to read this important message from all of our friends in the ocean.

Litter at the _____ is a big _____ for ocean life.
ECHAB   MERPLOB

But _____ like you can _____ a _____ of
    SDKI   KEMA   DOWLR

_____! Thank you for _____ putting _____
FERINECFED   YWAALS   TRETLI

where it _____ and never _____ even a little
         SONGLEB   IVALGEN

_____ of it _____ when you go _____.
TBI   HIBDEN   MEOH

Where did T-Rex take his vacation?

Answer: At the dino-shore.

49

⭐ Star Match

Do the math to match each sea star to its name.

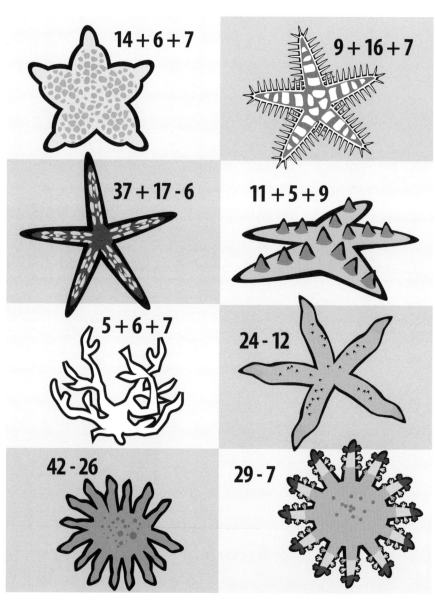

14 + 6 + 7

9 + 16 + 7

37 + 17 - 6

11 + 5 + 9

5 + 6 + 7

24 - 12

42 - 26

29 - 7

25 = chocolate chip star
22 = sun star
48 = candy cane star
18 = basket star

27 = cushion star
12 = fat star
32 = comb sea star
16 = sunflower sea star

A Galaxy of Sea Stars

There are more than 3,600 different kinds of sea stars. They come in lots of different colors and shapes. Some sea stars are colored to match the surfaces on which they live. This camouflage helps them hide from predators.

How many sea stars do you see?

Jumbo Word Search

Find the words by looking up, down, backwards, forwards, sideways, and diagonally.

```
P  T  C  S  H  O  R  E  S  P
H  E  E  S  Y  A  R  N  N  R
S  S  E  N  E  U  O  R  B  E
L  S  T  D  T  T  U  B  E  D
W  P  I  A  E  A  S  E  A  A
A  T  E  L  R  T  C  A  C  T
R  R  E  A  R  S  F  L  H  O
C  K  C  R  E  E  P  S  E  R
S  A  R  M  I  P  O  O  L  S
```

SEA	PREDATORS	CREEPS
STARS	CRAWLS	TIDE
SKELETONS	RAYS	POOL
TENTACLES	SHORE	ARM
CREATURE	TUBE	BEACH

Road Trip Journal

DATE:

PLACES WE WENT:

WHAT WE DID:

MY FAVORITE MEMORY OF THE DAY:

America's National Parks

Our nearly 400 national parks include canyons, mountains, monuments, battlefields, lakeshores, seashores, recreation areas, scenic rivers, trails, and historic sites. These parks are owned and managed by the American government — the government **of** the people and **by** the people. That means that the parks belong to **every** American!

Draw a star on this map to show approximately where you live. How many national parks are in your state?

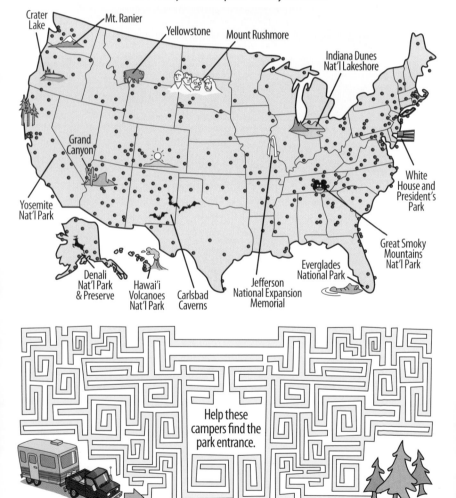

Crater Lake

Mt. Ranier

Yellowstone

Mount Rushmore

Indiana Dunes Nat'l Lakeshore

Grand Canyon

White House and President's Park

Yosemite Nat'l Park

Denali Nat'l Park & Preserve

Hawai'i Volcanoes Nat'l Park

Carlsbad Caverns

Jefferson National Expansion Memorial

Everglades National Park

Great Smoky Mountains Nat'l Park

Help these campers find the park entrance.

PARK RANGER KATE'S NATIONAL PARKS QUIZ

Do the math to discover the answers to these National Parks questions.

1. Which state is home to 24 national parks—more than any other state?

_____
$(9 + 13 + 7 + 6)$

2. What is the name of America's first national park?

_____
$(15 + 15 + 4 + 4)$

3. Just one U.S. state has no national parks. Which one is it?

_____
$(10 + 16 + 5 + 6)$

4. Which state has the largest national park (Wrangell-St. Elias National Park and Preserve, 13.2 million acres)?

_____
$(7 + 7 + 7 + 7 + 7 + 7)$

5. Which state is home to the smallest national park (Thaddeus Kosciuszko National Memorial, 0.02 acres)?

_____
$(7 + 6 + 7 + 6 + 7)$

6. Effigy Mounds National Historic Site has 195 prehistoric mounds, 31 of which are shaped like birds and animals. In which state can it be found?

_____
$(4 + 8 + 6 + 9 + 3)$

A N S W E R		K E Y	
42 = Alaska	**37** = Delaware	**33** = Pennsylvania
30 = Iowa	**35** = California	**38** = Yellowstone

Wildlife Fun & Fitness

Can you act like each of these kinds of animals found in America's national parks? It's great exercise!

Grizzly bears in Yellowstone can stand as tall as 7 to 8 feet on their hind legs.

TRY THIS: Pretend to be a grizzly waking up from hibernation. Curl up in a ball and then slowly stretch, stand, and reach your arms as high as you can.

Each summer evening, 400,000 Brazilian bats exit Carlsbad Caverns in search of insects for dinner.

TRY THIS: Run around your yard flapping your wings like a bat. Don't worry if you look a little batty!

Florida's Everglades National Park is home to many alligators. Their jaw muscles are incredibly powerful. Snap!

TRY THIS: Hold a bathroom scale in your hands. Squeeze as hard as you can. How many pounds of pressure can you apply?

The endangered gray wolf, the largest member of the canine family, can be found in national parks in Alaska.

TRY THIS: Wolves run in packs. Gather a group of friends and go for a run with your "pack."

Lookalike Lanterns

Look closely at these camping lanterns. Can you find the two that are identical?

What do you call a bear with no teeth?

Be a Junior Park Ranger

Many national parks offer young visitors the opportunity to join the National Parks Service family as Junior Park Rangers. Can you find the badge that's different from all the others?

Nature Walk Bingo

Head outdoors with family and friends and take a walk around the neighborhood. On this walk, each of you take one of the cards below and cross out the items as you see them. The first one to get three in a row yells, "Bingo!"

Jumbo Word Search

Find the words by looking up, down, backwards, forwards, sideways, and diagonally.

```
N O I T A E R C E R
D T H J R E V I L B
E L Y U G I A R A E
S C E N I C P D N R
I E A I Y S G O O U
T R U O F E K R I T
E S A R E A S R T A
S N A C I R E M A N
H I S T O R I C N P
```

RECREATION	JUNIOR	BADGE
NATIONAL	SCENIC	AREAS
AMERICAN	NATURE	FIELD
HISTORIC	PARKS	TRIP
RANGER	SITES	LIVE

Road Trip Journal

DATE:

PLACES WE WENT:

WHAT WE DID:

MY FAVORITE MEMORY OF THE DAY:

A Day at the Farm

Only two of these pigs are exact twins. Can you find them?

The Chicken and the Egg

Whether eaten alone or used as an ingredient in cooking, Americans eat about 240 eggs per person every year!

What's inside an egg?

Eggs are a great source of protein and contain 14 minerals and 11 vitamins. But when you eat an egg, do you ever look at it closely? Do the math to write in each part of the egg.

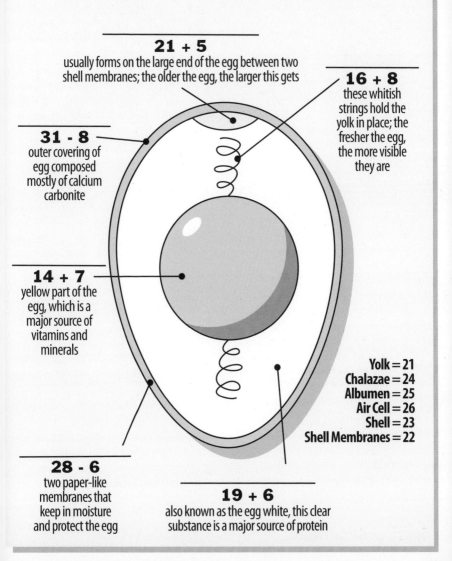

21 + 5
usually forms on the large end of the egg between two shell membranes; the older the egg, the larger this gets

16 + 8
these whitish strings hold the yolk in place; the fresher the egg, the more visible they are

31 - 8
outer covering of egg composed mostly of calcium carbonite

14 + 7
yellow part of the egg, which is a major source of vitamins and minerals

28 - 6
two paper-like membranes that keep in moisture and protect the egg

19 + 6
also known as the egg white, this clear substance is a major source of protein

Yolk = 21
Chalazae = 24
Albumen = 25
Air Cell = 26
Shell = 23
Shell Membranes = 22

Farm Fractions

Locally grown fruits and vegetables are usually harvested within 24 hours of being purchased. They are the freshest and most nutritious.

What fraction of this local garden is each type of vegetable is growing in?

CARROTS: ⬜ —

BROCCOLI: ⬜ —

PUMPKINS: ⬜ —

TOMATOES: ⬜ —

Corny Facts

REPLACE THE MISSING WORDS

First grown in Mexico over 10,000 _____ ago, there are over 3,500 different corn products. Corn is one of the most popular _____ in the USA and is sold fresh, canned, or _____. Think of all the different ways you might _____ corn: sweet corn, popcorn, chips, tortillas, polenta, cornmeal, grits, oil, and syrup. Corn mixed with lima _____ is called *succotash*. Only _____ type of corn can become popcorn. Field corn and sweet corn will not _____.

YEARS
VEGGIES
EAT POP FROZEN
ONE BEANS

Popcorn Taste Test

Ask a parent to make some plain popcorn. Divide it into four bowls and compare these flavors.

CLASSIC
Top one bowl with melted butter and a little salt. Simple, but it's a movie theater favorite.

CHEESY
Sprinkle popcorn with three tablespoons of Parmesan cheese and mix.

SWEET
Mash a banana in a bowl. Add popcorn. Drizzle honey over the popcorn. Mix gently.

SPICY
Make a little mix of chili powder, cumin, and black pepper. Sprinkle on popcorn (but go easy at first!)

Color the Cows

Holsteins

Holsteins are white with black spots. Holsteins are used because they give a lot of milk. Did you know that no two Holsteins have the same spot pattern? Color the Holstein.

Jerseys

Jerseys are light brown and have big, pretty eyes. Jerseys give less milk than Holsteins, but their milk contains more cream. Their milk is often used for cheese. Color the Jersey.

Guernseys

Guernseys are brown and white. They are known for their sweet personalities. Color the Guernsey.

One cow will produce about 200,000 glasses of milk in her lifetime. Cows drink 25 to 50 gallons of water a day—enough to fill your bathtub!

Dairy Farm Crossword

Complete the crossword by filling in a word for each clue.

Across

2. A very young cow
4. America's favorite ice cream flavor
7. A cow stores her milk here
8. The U.S. Department of Agriculture recommends kids get this number of dairy servings daily
9. Tastes great on corn

Down

1. The most popular flavor of milk
2. Milk mineral that keeps bones strong
3. Milk is approximately 97 percent _____
5. This is National Dairy Month
6. Cows graze on this

Little Miss Muffet Mystery

Little Miss Muffet sat on a tuffet
Eating her curds and whey . . .

You've heard this nursery rhyme many times, but what exactly are **curds** and **whey?**

Replace the missing words in the article below.

How does milk become cheese?

MILK CONTAINS PRESSED QUICKLY BITS CHEESE

Milk in a glass looks like a liquid. But it is actually a liquid that contains lots of solid _____ of protein.

When milk gets old, or when a little acid is added, the bits of protein bond together and form clumps called **curds**. If you've ever eaten cottage _____, then you have eaten curds.

The leftover liquid is called **whey**.

From curds to cheese

Before refrigerators, _____ would spoil _____. Back then, people stored milk in bags made from a cow's stomach. The inside of a cow's stomach _____ an acid called **rennet** which makes the milk form curds. Over time, people discovered that when curds were _____ together to remove the liquid whey, the milk curds became a solid cheese.

68

Smile and Say "Cheese!"

You probably know that milk is used to make cheese. But did you know that about one-third of the milk produced in the U.S. is used to make cheese? Wisconsin is the top cheesemaker state, producing two and a half billion pounds of cheese every year.

Find the two identical slices of cheese.

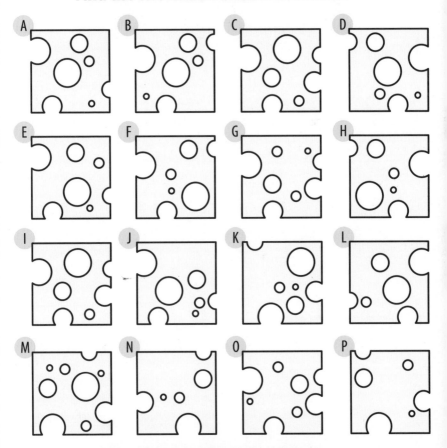

Cheesy Champion

Circle every other letter to discover which kind of cheese is America's top seller.

Q (M) S O C Z B Z N A P R O E G L M L N A

M _ _ _ _ _ _ _ _ _

Jumbo Word Search

Find the words by looking up, down, backwards, forwards, sideways, and diagonally.

```
P  P  T  O  R  R  A  C  F  K
U  T  O  P  S  L  P  H  L  A
M  Y  R  P  B  A  M  I  L  M
P  T  R  U  C  R  M  C  G  S
K  O  M  I  A  O  T  K  A  T
I  E  E  F  A  T  R  E  A  I
N  Y  O  L  K  D  B  N  L  R
S  U  C  C  O  T  A  S  H  G
E  S  N  I  E  T  S  L  O  H
```

SUCCOTASH	POPCORN	PIG
HOLSTEINS	CARROT	LIMA
CHICKEN	GRITS	MILK
ALBUMEN	DAIRY	SPOT
PUMPKINS	FARM	YOLK

Road Trip Journal

DATE: _____

PLACES WE WENT: _____

_____

_____

_____

WHAT WE DID: _____

_____

_____

_____

_____

_____

_____

_____

_____

_____

MY FAVORITE MEMORY OF THE DAY: _____

_____

_____

_____

_____

_____

_____

ANSWERS

Page 6

Page 7
License Plate Literacy

Smile For Me
Awesome Teacher
You Are Great
Love to Travel
Good to Be Me
Fun to Learn
Dream Bigger
Happy Kidz

Page 8
North American Road Trip

Kansas
Saskatchewan
Kentucky
Texas

Page 9

Wyoming
Oregon
Quebec

Page 10
The World's Longest Maze

Hawaii

Page 11
Minivan Matchup

D & E

Page 12

Page 16
Balloon Pop

Katie got the highest score
143 odd, 132 even

Page 17
Livestock Scramble

COW

RABBIT

PIG

TURKEY

LAMB

CHICKEN

Page 18
Pie Baking Contest

Judge's Score Card
Color	⊞	6
Aroma	⊠	9
Texture	⊠	7
Flavor	⊠	9
TOTAL		**31**

Judge's Score Card
Color	⊟	5
Aroma	◹	4
Texture	◨	8
Flavor	⊞	6
TOTAL		**23**

Judge's Score Card
Color	⊠	7
Texture	◨	8
Texture	⊞	6
Flavor	⊠	9
TOTAL		**30**

Page 19

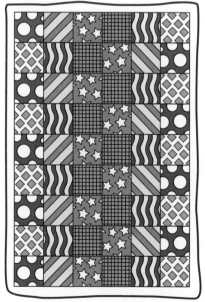

Page 20

Page 22
How many sunglasses can you find on this page?
20

Protect Your Skin!
Wear a hat
Wear a shirt over your swimsuit
Stay in the shade
Use sunscreeen

Page 23

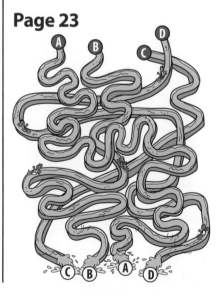

Page 24

Amazing Water Parks

The Wisconsin Dells boasts more than twenty indoor and outdoor water parks. They hold a combined total of **16** million gallons of water.

Noah's Ark, located in the Dells, is America's largest water park. It covers **70** acres with three miles of water slides.

A water slide at the Atlantis resort in the Bahamas features a **60** foot slide with a clear tube through a shark pool!

The world's largest indoor wave pool is in Edmonton, Canada. The tropical oasis there has an average temperature of **31**°C (88°F).

Deep River Waterpark in Indiana has its own ice-skating rink. You must be **46** inches tall to ride the Dragon Speed Rides.

Cedar Point Shores Waterpark in Sandusky, Ohio has a ride with a **6** story drop where riders free fall to the pool below.

Page 25

How many pool noodles do you see?

37

Page 28

Page 30

Porcupines: A Prickle
Skunks: A Surfeit
Squirrels: A Scurry
Foxes: A Leash
Elk: A Gang
Bats: A Colony

Page 31

Page 32
Camp Confusion
D & F

Page 33
Put Out That Campfire!

Page 34
Who is walking in the woods?
rabbit: 17 - 7 = 10
raccoon: 19 - 6 = 13
squirrel: 23 - 7 = 16
deer: 18 - 4 = 14
bear: 21 - 6 = 15

Page 35
General Sherman Tree is a Record Breaker!
The tree is estimated to be **2,500** years old.

It weighs **642** tons.

It's **275** feet (83m) tall.

The distance around the bottom of the tree is **102** feet (31m).

It has branches that are almost **7** feet (2.1m) in diameter.

Page 36

Page 38
What hippopotamus means
River horse

Page 39
Monkey See, Monkey Do
2 & 13

Page 40
Chameleon Cutie
2012

Dwarf Three-Toed Jerboa
Cotton Ball

Page 41
What are pangolins?
Pangolins are mammals.

Page 42
Which giraffe is the tallest?
Amare: 21 feet tall
Jafari: 14 feet tall
Feechi: 18 feel tall

Page 43
What do Tasmanian devils eat?
We are carnivores. That means we eat **MEAT**. And we're also scavengers, which means we mostly eat dead or dying animals we **FIND**.

SCIENTISTS believe that Tasmanian devils were once good runners. But since the **INVENTION** of cars, we get plenty of food by eating the animals that get run over. So, we don't have to cover large **DISTANCES** searching for food like we did back in the old days.

Page 44

Page 46
A Day at the Beach
L

Page 47
Bummer, Dude

Page 48
Surfboard Scramble
A & F

Page 49
Super Sea-cret Message
Litter at the **BEACH** is a big **PROBLEM** for ocean life. But **KIDS** like you can **MAKE** a **WORLD** of **DIFFERENCE**! Thank you for **ALWAYS** putting **LITTER** where it **BELONGS** and never **LEAVING** even a little **BIT** of it **BEHIND** when you go **HOME**.

Page 50
Star Match

27 = cushion star
32 = comb sea star
48 = candy cane star
25 = chocolate chip star
18 = basket star
12 = fat star
16 = sunflower sea star
22 = sun star

Page 51
A Galaxy of Sea Stars
14

Page 52

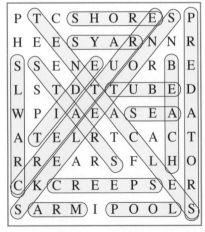

Page 54

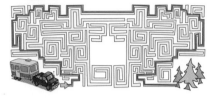

Page 55
National Parks Quiz
1. California
2. Yellowstone
3. Delaware
4. Alaska
5. Pennsylvania
6. Iowa

Page 57
Lookalike Lanterns
G & I

Page 58
Be a Junior Park Ranger
I

Page 60

Page 62
A Day at the Farm
M & H

Page 63
What's inside an egg?

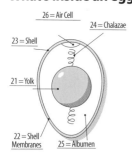

- 26 = Air Cell
- 24 = Chalazae
- 23 = Shell
- 21 = Yolk
- 22 = Shell Membranes
- 25 = Albumen

Page 64
Farm Fractions

 CARROTS: $\frac{1}{4}$ BROCCOLI: $\frac{1}{16}$

PUMPKINS: $\frac{1}{2}$ TOMATOES: $\frac{3}{16}$

Page 65
Corny Facts

First grown in Mexico over 10,000 **YEARS** ago, there are over 3,500 different corn products. Corn is one of the most popular **VEGGIES** in the USA and is sold fresh, canned, or **FROZEN**. Think of all the different ways you might **EAT** corn: sweet corn, popcorn, chips, tortillas, polenta, cornmeal, grits, oil, and syrup. Corn mixed with lima **BEANS** is called *succotash*. Only **ONE** type of corn can become popcorn. Field corn and sweet corn will not **POP**.

Page 67
Dairy Farm Crossword

Across	Down
2. Calf	1. Chocolate
4. Vanilla	2. Calcium
7. Udder	3. Water
8. Three	5. June
9. Butter	6. Grass

Page 68
How does milk become cheese?

Milk in a glass looks like a liquid. But it is actually a liquid that contains lots of solid **BITS** of protein.

When milk gets old, or when a little acid is added, the bits of protein bond together and form clumps called curds. If you've ever eaten cottage **CHEESE**, then you have eaten curds.

The leftover liquid is called whey.

From curds to cheese

Before refrigerators, **MILK** would spoil **QUICKLY**. Back then, people stored milk in bags made from a cow's stomach. The inside of a cow's stomach **CONTAINS** an acid called rennet which makes the milk form curds. Over time, people discovered that when curds were **PRESSED** together to remove the liquid whey, the milk curds became a solid cheese.

Page 69
Smile and Say "Cheese!"

C & I

Cheesy Champion

Mozzarella

Page 70

Who made this book?

Super Fun Road Trip Activities for Kids was made by the people who bring the weekly *Kid Scoop* page to hundreds of newspapers!

When Fox Chapel discovered Kid Scoop, they knew that there were lots of kids looking for books just like this one.

***Kid Scoop* believes learning is fun!** Our educational activity pages teach and entertain. Teachers use the page in schools to promote standards-based learning. Parents use the *Kid Scoop* materials to foster academic success, a joy of learning, and family discussions. Our fun puzzles and activities draw children into the page. This stimulates a child's interest and they then read the text.

Vicki Whiting – Author

Vicki was a third-grade teacher for many years. Now she loves teaching kids through the weekly entertaining and educational *Kid Scoop* page. People often ask where she gets her ideas for each week's page. Vicki says, "I listen to the questions kids ask. We answer those questions with every *Kid Scoop* page!"

Jeff Schinkel – Illustrator

Jeff has loved to draw his whole life! As a kid, sometimes he was drawing when he should have been listening to the teacher in class. He earned a BFA in Illustration at the Academy of Art University in San Francisco, where drawing in class is highly encouraged. Jeff is now a member of the National Cartoonists Society.

Vivien Whittington – Operations Manager

Vivien is a voracious reader! She always wanted to work in publishing and after getting a degree in Fine Art, worked in publishing houses in London, England, starting as a researcher and leaving as a senior editor. Vivien coordinates the *Kid Scoop* team to complete around 50 different page deadlines a month—like an air traffic controller!

Eli Smith – Graphic Designer, Webmaster

Eli grew up in Cazadero, California, population 420, near the Russian River. He received a graphics degree from Santa Rosa Junior College and became interested in visual arts through his father, who is a painter. Eli is an accomplished photographer and spends weekends hiking and photographing the hills and beaches of Sonoma County.

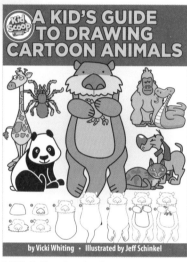

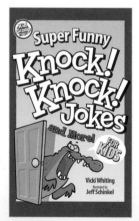